IT was a bitter night in January. A wind from the north piled the snow into drifts so deep they reached to the eaves of the little house in Litchfield where a first child had just been born to Joseph and Mary Baker Allen.

Litchfield was in a wild part of the old colony of Connecticut. On the night the Allen child was born, the howling of wolves could be heard plain enough in the surrounding forest, while an owl called mournfully from a great pine tree. Yet the Allens were snug, for maple logs burned in the big fireplace and the cellar was filled with good things to eat. In the barn the cattle and sheep were bedded down, warm with straw.

"Let the wolves howl as they will," said Mr. Allen. "We are safe and comfortable, and now we must find a name for our son." So he did what nearly all new fathers did in 1737 in Connecticut — took down the big Bible from its place on the mantel and turned the pages slowly, looking at them closely by the dancing flames of the open fire. "I have it," said he at last. "Mary, we will call him Ethan."

In this simple way Ethan Allen was named. If the night was wild and the wolves noisy, it was only proper, for Ethan Allen was to live a life filled with storms. He was to be a man given to violent actions and language, yet a truer or braver man never lived.

Shortly after he was born the Allen family moved to Cornwall, a town so new that the settlers had to hew their homes out of the deep forest, and plant corn between the stumps.

In Cornwall five more sons and two daughters were born to the Allens, and their names were also

chosen from the Bible. There was Heman and
Heber and Levi and Zimri and Ira; and the girls,
Lucy and Lydia. Gradually, the Allen home, at
first only a one-room house with the earth for a
floor and a broad tree stump for a table, was enlarged.
The boys cleared more land and planted it, harvest-
ing corn and buckwheat and potatoes. The girls
made butter, and learned to spin woolen yarn,
which they wove into cloth to make clothes for
themselves and their brothers.

All of the boys were good hunters and fishermen.
They had to be if the family were to eat well, and
eat well they did, three heavy meals a day. For one
noonday dinner in September, Lucy supplied rasp-
berries and Lydia made a great bowl of applesauce.
Heman furnished a long string of brook trout, which

6

were fried in corn meal ground by Heber and Levi from whole grain. Zimri cleaned and plucked six fine partridges he had shot, which Mother Allen rolled in mud, then baked. To young Ira went the job of digging new potatoes from among the stumps. As for the oldest, Ethan, he had taken his gun and gone into the forest before daylight, to return in midmorning with a buck deer.

7

Ethan was a superb woodsman, but also, of all the children, he showed the most liking for books. When he had read the Bible, he finished the few other books in the Allen household, then borrowed from neighbors. Father Allen had always been a great reader and he was pleased that his son showed the makings of a scholar.

One day when Mr. Allen and Ethan were building fence, the older man spoke of what was on his mind. "Ethan," he said, "do you think you would like to go to college?"

The young man was astonished. Why, he had never known but two men who had gone to a college. "Father," he cried, "would it be possible? When?"

"I have spoken to the Reverend Jonathan Lee over in Salisbury about it. He will prepare you for Yale College."

"But how can we pay him?"

"I shall pay him in cash and in provisions as I can. And you are to live there and to work about his place. He will instruct you every day."

Ethan was delighted at the idea of reading all he wanted and of becoming a learned man, such as Mr. Lee, who was said to read both Greek and Latin. Packing his few belongings in a bundle he struck out on foot for Salisbury, several miles through the deep woods.

Mr. Lee found Ethan an apt pupil, and the young

man discovered Mr. Lee to be an excellent, if strict, teacher. All was going well when a terrible blow came. Father Allen died suddenly. His passing deprived Ethan of a kindly parent and also of an education. His boyhood was over. He must take his father's place as head of the family.

Young Ethan was already a strong, tall man, the tallest person in Cornwall. His mind was active. He had energy to burn. Taking charge of the farm work, he directed his brothers in cutting wood, in plowing and planting. He also turned out to be good at business. Discovering that a man named Joseph Mather had owed his father a sum of money, he went to Mr. Mather and asked for the cash.

"I haven't got it," said Mr. Mather, a surly fellow.

11

Ethan stood up tall and big and an angry cloud passed over his face. "You'd better get it and soon," he growled. "I have eight people to feed and clothe."

"How can I pay when I haven't got the money?"

"Give me food."

"All I have is some buckwheat."

"That will do. I'll take twelve bushels and call it square."

Mr. Mather did not really intend to give up the buckwheat, but he looked again at the big young man with the flashing eyes. "All right," he said, "you can take it now."

Ethan proved a good trader, swapping farm produce for things the family needed and could not make or grow, things like salt and pepper, and occasionally some tea.

Meanwhile, war had broken out between France and England. Both countries wanted the American colonies. Connecticut was said to be in danger of attack by the French. So, in 1757, when he was still not twenty, Ethan turned the farm over to his brothers and joined a militia regiment raised to defend a fort against the French.

Ethan was to see little of war — this time. He did a lot of marching through new country, then went home. But he had decided not to be a farmer. Just what he did want to do, he didn't know. It

12

must be something as exciting as possible.

Over in Salisbury, where he had gone to school to Mr. Lee, was a big hill that was said to contain iron ore. For a little cash Ethan got the right to mine it. He set about building a blast furnace in which to smelt the ore into pure iron. Hiring a few men, and directing them with great bustle, he was soon making iron and running it into molds to make big kettles.

Ethan had figured shrewdly. All over Connecticut men were beginning to make potash from which soap and other things could be manufactured. To make potash, big kettles were needed. And now Ethan Allen was ready to supply the market.

With money coming in, Ethan thought of marriage. Mary Brownson, daughter of a miller to whom Ethan used to take corn and buckwheat to be ground, was the girl. Mary said "yes" to his question, and they were married in Cornwall.

Making their home near the blast furnace in Salisbury, the Allens were very happy. Ethan still found time to read a good deal, and here in Salisbury was just the man he needed to make up for his lost education. He was Doctor Thomas Young, a medical graduate of Yale College, who rode the poor roads and trails of the town on horseback, giving out medicine to the sick. Doctor Young liked to talk and he was an original thinker. He owned by far

13

the biggest collection of books in town, and Ethan borrowed and read every one of them, meantime learning much from his long conversations with the brilliant and kindly physician.

But scholarly though he was, Ethan was also a hot-headed youth. In an argument over a business deal, he and George Caldwell, a fellow townsman, got into a row, and Caldwell complained to the constable that Ethan had attacked him. The officer came to take Ethan to court.

"What am I charged with?" Ethan demanded.

"You are charged," said the officer, "with assault and battery on the person of George Caldwell and in the presence and to the disturbance of his majesty's good subjects."

"Caldwell attacked me. I only defended myself."

"You'd better come along, anyway."

Taken before Judge Hutchinson, that grave man decided the disturbance against His Majesty's good subjects was worth ten shillings. Ethan paid the fine.

Selling out his iron business, Ethan looked around for something to do. He wanted to get away, he said, to do something new, something different than he had been doing. There was a lot of talk going around about the wild region north of Connecticut

14

colony. Not much was known of it other than
that the governor of New Hampshire was selling
land very cheaply up there. The region was gen-
erally known as the New Hampshire Grants.

Only a few brave souls had seen this distant
northern country. It was said to be full of game
and fish, now becoming scarce in Connecticut. Its
forests, so Ethan heard, were of wonderful pine, and
its steep hills were so well covered with timber they
were called Green Mountains. It sounded to Ethan
like a good country.

Always a man of quick action, Ethan called
brothers Heman and Levi into conference. "I am
going up and look over the New Hampshire Grants,"
he said.

"What's the idea?" asked Heman.

15

"I think it might be a good place, maybe, to start a new colony."

"What's the matter with Connecticut?"

"Oh, the people are becoming too thick. These settlements are too close together. I want room."

"I hear it's pretty cold up there on the Grants," put in Levi.

"Well, it's winter right now," said Ethan. "A good time to find out how cold it is."

"Think you can find your way around?"

"Find my way around?" Ethan exploded. "Why, I could find my way clean to Canada, if I wanted to go there."

Taking a hunting knife, a gun, a powder horn, with flint and steel, and a pocketful of dried venison, Ethan strapped on his snowshoes and said good-bye to his brothers and his wife and child.

"Mary," he told his wife, "I think that is good country up on the Grants. Maybe I will find a place for us to settle on the frontier."

"I don't know whether I'd like to be so far from home."

"You wait and see. We can have land for almost nothing up there."

Ethan Allen had become one of the best woodsmen in America. Now he traveled a hundred miles into the deep pine forest, making camp at night under a windfall of branches, cooking game

16

that he shot, noting the streams and the hills, the fine
pines and spruces, the groves of great maples, and
the ridges of fine beech. He was enchanted with
this great wilderness, with its hush, broken only by
the melancholy cry of the owl, and the howls of
wolves and bobcats.

For many days he traveled without seeing a human
being or a house. And then a fierce blizzard came
on suddenly. His clothes were damp. Knowing
that he might well freeze to death if he stopped
moving, and unable to find any natural shelter from
the storm, Ethan marked out a path in a circle and
walked it all night. Long before morning his power-
ful body became woefully tired, and he staggered
and even fell a few times. Each time, however, he
managed to get to his feet.

18

The storm let up about daylight. Ethan had survived. Now that he could see, he found a spot under some thick pines where the snow had not penetrated. Digging with his hands he scooped together a mass of dry pine needles. With his knife he cut dead branches from trees, and soon he had a brisk fire going, hot enough to thaw out his clothes and to warm his dried venison. In later years he told how he had never been quite so near death as that night in the blizzard.

Yet he had fallen in love with this new, untouched region, and by the time he was home again in Connecticut, he knew that he wanted to move to the Grants.

Ethan Allen could hardly have known what a violent place the New Hampshire Grants were soon

19

to become. When he first saw the country, it was all silent except for the calls of the wild birds and animals and the sighing of wind in the pines.

It was soon going to be changed from solitude to a storm of troubles by the King of England, who did not know very much about his colonies in America. For one thing, he had permitted the governor of New Hampshire to sell land west of the Connecticut River. For another, he had permitted the governor of New York to sell land eastward from the Hudson to the Connecticut River.

Many Connecticut men, including friends of Ethan Allen, had bought lands on the Grants from New Hampshire. Other men, in New York, had bought the same lands from their governor.

Everyone knows that two men cannot each own the same piece of ground. By the time Ethan had returned from his winter trip, a number of Connecticut men were worried. They had bought New Hampshire land on the Grants. Some had already moved to settle there. Others were planning to do so. But now they were told by the governor of New York that their lands had been sold elsewhere, especially in large tracts to New York land speculators — people who bought and sold land to make money not to live on.

Not long after his trip through the Grants, a group of Connecticut men called on him.

20

"Ethan," said the spokesman, "you know what is going on about our lands up there?"

"I think I do. They have been sold two ways."

"That's it. We men here paid cash for our lands to Governor Wentworth of New Hampshire. Now New York claims we have no right to them."

"It is a case, gentlemen, of speculation by the wealthy men of New York."

"They themselves are not going to live on the Grants."

"Not they," growled Ethan. "They will not even see the lands they claim to have bought."

"We know that. But what can we do to hold the lands we have paid for?"

"Sirs, you can fight for them."

"But the courts are slow."

"Hang the courts! I mean fight, *fight* — unless you are sheep."

There was silence for a moment, then Ethan, his brow darkening, his eyes squinting, spoke again.

"Gentlemen," he fairly roared, "you can't defend your titles until you get busy. The Yorkers are up there right now!"

There was more talk, and the groups went away with plans to meet soon again, well satisfied that they had found a staunch man in rugged young Ethan Allen.

The next meeting was held one day in March, 1770, in a tavern at Canaan, Connecticut. Ethan was there by invitation. The group agreed for each man to pay a sum of money into a fund to be used to defend their land titles against the Yorkers. Ethan was to act for the group. He was to use the courts, they instructed him, or, if the courts failed to act, any other method that seemed best.

Calling for his horse immediately, Ethan mounted in front of the tavern. "My friends," he cried in tones that shook the window panes, "I am on my way to Portsmouth to talk to Governor Wentworth. If he can do nothing to help us, I shall act. . . ." Waving his hat, he slapped his steed and away he galloped on the trail northward, while the Connecticut men cheered.

24

At Portsmouth Ethan got copies of the deeds to the lands sold on the Grants by New Hampshire. He also bought a tract for himself. While riding back to Connecticut, he learned that the governor of New York had just issued a proclamation ordering all New Hampshire settlers on the Grants to give up their lands and leave, or be ejected (thrown out) by the New York officers. By now some thirty or more Connecticut families had actually settled on the Grants. They had made clearings for their fields. Gardens were growing. Fences had been put up. Cabins and barns had been built.

Ethan hired the best lawyer he could find in Connecticut and rode fast to Albany, in New York, where the hearings for ejectment were to be held. The judges, all New York men, quickly decided in favor of the New York claimants. Ethan was more than disappointed. He was very angry. Then one of the Yorkers came to him.

"Mr. Allen," said he, "if you will aid the New York cause, we shall be glad to give you, free, a large parcel of land on the Grants."

"Sir," Ethan spoke indignantly, "I represent the genuine settlers, the poor people who are living there. I want none of *your* land."

"Mr. Allen," the Yorker spoke very sternly, 'you should be advised that your people already on the Grants will do well to deal with *us*. We Yorkers

are the rightful landlords. We have might on our side and you know that might often makes right."

Ethan was getting hot under the collar, but he held his temper well. "Sir," he replied, just as sternly as the other, "the gods of the hills are not the gods of the valleys."

The Yorker did not understand. "What do you mean?" he asked.

"Come with me to the Grants," answered Ethan, "and what I mean will become clear." It was obviously some sort of threat. Ethan followed it up. "Our country people on the Grants," said he, "do not understand your complicated and unfair city laws. But they do understand they have paid for the lands they are living on."

"They are mistaken."

27

"Perhaps, sir, you Yorkers are mistaken. Do you think that a man who has cut his home out of the savage woods, who has made corn grow among the stumps is to be driven off by words?"

With that, Ethan Allen mounted his horse and rode back to the Grants to the new village of Bennington. On the way he thought over the problem. These Yorkers were simply owners of huge grants of land which they meant to sell. Not one of them planned to settle on the land they claimed. It was quite different with Ethan's group of small farmers. More were already coming to the Grants to add to the thirty pioneer families.

On arriving at Bennington Ethan was met by the settlers in the new tavern built by Landlord Stephen Fay. It was called "The Catamount," and to show that Landlord Fay was on the side of the settlers headed by Ethan Allen, a stuffed catamount, or mountain lion, crouched on a pole outside the door. The animal's mouth was open in a snarl with its glittering teeth showing in the direction of New York.

Ethan was delighted with the big cat. "Show your teeth!" he shouted as he drove up. "Show your teeth and snarl! By the gods of the hills I swear that Yorkers shall not steal our lands by the trickery of courts!"

The settlers gathered around the tall young man

28

whose voice could carry almost a full mile. "Boys," he shouted, "boys, we've got to organize a regiment of fighting men if we are going to hold our lands."

Landlord Fay spoke up. "Do you think they will try to put us out by force?"

"By force?" shouted Ethan. "By force? Of course they will. They will drive us off like so many wolves — if we don't protect ourselves."

"Well, why *don't* we protect ourselves?" It was Peleg Sunderland who spoke, a tough old Indian fighter, a man who knew the woods and the rivers, who liked bear meat for breakfast.

"Yes, let's have an army," put in Levi Allen, now come to live on the Grants. His huge brother Ethan looked over the men present, his wild eyes flashing with the idea of a backwoods army. "Come," he rumbled, "let us get busy."

Then and there, in the Catamount Tavern, Ethan Allen formed a company of fighting men, a small army whose soldiers all swore they would be ready to meet at a moment's notice to defend the farms of all New Hampshire settlers.

Ethan Allen was elected colonel. His chief officer was his cousin, Seth Warner. Among the rank and file were brothers Levi and Ira, and the seasoned old Indian fighter, Peleg Sunderland.

Yorker spies in Bennington quickly got word to the governor of New York, reporting that Allen had raised a company of men and was drilling them. The governor boiled over. He swore that he would drive those bad men into the Green Mountains.

Ethan, always quick to sense the value of good publicity, was elated. "Men," he cried, "the Yorker governor has named us. We are the "Green Mountain Boys!""

But the governor was not fooling. Soon on his order came Yorker Sheriff Ten Eyck and a posse of three hundred men, all armed, to evict a settler named Breakenridge. Word of his coming was brought on ahead by a New Hampshire man, and young Jonas Fay, son of the Catamount landlord, sent runners speeding to the scattered farms.

"A wolf hunt, a wolf hunt!" shouted the runners. "A wolf hunt at the Breakenridge place "

This was all the news that was needed. Young men in buckskin took down their long guns from over fireplaces, and quickly gathered near the Break-

enridge farm, all unknown to the Yorker sheriff and his crew. The Green Mountain Boys signaled to each other by imitating bird calls, and presently had taken places where they could cover the farm with their guns.

When Sheriff Ten Eyck and his three hundred men moved into the Breakenridge clearing, they saw that the cabin was well barricaded and the log walls pierced with mean-looking loopholes, each just large enough for a gun barrel.

In the Breakenridge field were forty men with guns across their arms. This reception did not look very encouraging to the sheriff, but he marched on until he came to the edge of the field. Here he was stopped by seven of the waiting men.

"Out of my way!" roared the sheriff. "I am here to enforce the laws of the colony of New York."

"The laws of New York do not apply in the Green Mountains," growled one of the seven.

"Go back to New York where you belong," said another.

But after a brief discussion the sheriff was permitted to advance to a spot near the house, where Farmer Breakenridge came out to meet him. The sheriff read the order of eviction.

"That paper means nothing to me," said the resolute farmer. "I am under protection of the town

32

of Bennington and her Green Mountain Boys."
He waved his hand toward the armed men in the
field, who stood silent and sinister and ready. Breakenridge waved his hand again, and the sheriff noted
something he had not seen before: the heads and guns
of what looked to be another hundred or more men,
peering down from the top of a ridge above the
field.

It was a tough spot, but the sheriff was equal to
it. He returned to his army and gave orders to
advance. But the men did not have the spirit
needed to move under the guns of those half-hidden
men on the ridge. They started to fall away, first
in two's and three's, then by the dozen. But the
brave sheriff and some twenty men walked toward
the cabin.

"Open the door or I'll batter it down!" he shouted.

It was a tense moment. Just then the sheriff heard what sounded like an order given in the woods on the ridge, followed by clicking noises. In one glance the Yorker saw that the forty men in the field had leveled their guns at him, while another hundred guns were trained from the ridge. Sheriff Ten Eyck knew when he was beaten. Letting go a loud curse, he and his remaining crew turned and went away.

The Green Mountain Boys had won their first battle without a shot.

New York had not given up, however. One day word came to Colonel Ethan Allen that a Yorker surveyor by the name of Cockburn and a party

were running lines on the Grants. Two days later
Surveyor Cockburn and men were startled by a
gang dressed like Indians, even to stained faces.
The biggest of these fake savages, who was very
tall, did the talking and it wasn't in Indian but in
rousing good Yankee.

"Get off the Grants!" he roared. "Do you hear?
Get off the Grants and back to New York, or we'll
cut off your ears, you and all your gang!"

"I was sent here by the governor of New York."

"We Indians do not understand Yorker talk,"
replied the tall savage.

"But I must finish my work here."

"You want to lose your ears, then? Begone, I
tell you, and now!"

Cockburn and his party left, to report in Albany
that the Grants were fast becoming unsafe.

Ethan and his men returned to the Catamount
Tavern, where they washed the bark stain off their
faces.

Now, there was trouble close at home. It was a
Bennington man, Doctor Adams, and he said that
New York had a right to the Grants and all they
contained. He armed himself, too, and vowed that
any Green Mountain Boys who bothered *him* would
be shot dead.

This would never do. Colonel Allen sent a squad

of his men to bring the doctor to "court" at the
Catamount Inn. They took him without a shot
and brought him before the Colonel.

"You are a miserable Yorker!" Colonel Allen
shouted at him, and then pretended to hold a trial.
Doctor Adams was of course found guilty of
"treason."

"Truss him up beneath the big cat," Judge Allen
ordered, and the Boys tied the protesting doctor in
a chair and hoisted him up under the stuffed catamount sign, where he was left suspended for an hour
while children jeered him for being a dirty old
Yorker. No more talk was heard from Doctor
Adams.

There was more work elsewhere. Yorker agents
were moving into the Grants and had begun a settle-

ment they called New Perth, centered around the house and barn of a man named Hutchinson. Early one morning, just as daylight was faintly showing, terrifying cries sounded from the woods around New Perth, and then from all sides Green Mountain Boys swept into the clearing. Leading the raid was Colonel Ethan Allen, with Lieutenants Robert Cochran and Remember Baker.

Hutchinson and his hired men came tumbling out of the cabin to meet Colonel Allen.

"Out of your hovels!" roared Allen. "Get your cattle out of their barn, too — unless you want them burned."

"You have no right, you . . ."

"Turn out the cows, boys," shouted Colonel Allen. "Then fire the barn."

"But New York has its rights here."

"New York has nothing to do hereabouts."

Smoke was rising from the barn.

"The cabin is next, Hutchinson. Get your stuff out."

Still protesting, Hutchinson and his men carried things out of the doomed cabin, and a moment later it was in flames.

When all the buildings had been burned, Allen spoke to the Yorker settler. "Go your way now," he said, "and take your complaints to that scoundrel, the governor of New York.

39

Hutchinson hurried to Albany where he reported the outrage to the governor. Promptly New York posted a reward of twenty pounds or about a hundred dollars each for the arrest of Ethan Allen, Remember Baker, Robert Cochran, and two others who had taken leading parts in the raid on New Perth.

Drinking cider with several of the Boys in the Catamount, Ethan had an idea. "I think," he said, "I shall ride to Albany and see if anybody dares to try to collect the reward."

"Don't do that, Ethan," protested Landlord Fay. "They might catch you, and you can't help us if you are in a Yorker jail."

"They won't catch me. Fetch my horse."

While waiting for the animal, Ethan noticed a bushel bag full of salt near the tavern door. Without

42

a word he leaned over, took the bag's top in his strong teeth and with a mighty heave threw the heavy sack up and over his shoulder, never touching his hands to it. "Do you think any Yorker will want to bother with ME?" he laughed as he mounted his horse. The crowd could hear him still roaring with laughter as he passed out of sight.

Riding straight to Albany, Ethan entered the largest tavern in the town. Right in front of him, back of the bar, was one of the posters offering a reward for Allen and the other Boys. Ethan ordered a glass of rum and stood drinking, meanwhile reading the poster.

"Twenty pounds is a lot of money," he observed to the tavern keeper.

"It isn't too much to pay for outlaws like that

43

scoundrel, Ethan Allen."

"What makes him so bad?"

"Why, he's raiding farms on the Grants, burning, murdering, committing every crime."

"Must be a terrible man."

"He is a terrible man, a dangerous man, and he must be caught."

Ethan peered closely at the poster. "This doesn't give any description of him. What does he look like?"

"Oh, I know him well. He's a great big fellow."

"How big? As big as me?"

The tavern keeper laughed. "He's twice as big as you," he said.

"Well, well, that's pretty big." Ethan finished his rum, talked a while with several loungers, then mounted his horse and returned to Bennington. The incident, which he related in the Catamount, made him more famous than ever, even though Landlord Fay said it had been a foolish piece of bravado.

Ethan Allen now moved his own family from Connecticut to the Grants, and for the next three years lived as an outlaw. So did many of the Green Mountain Boys. They continued to evict Yorkers who came to settle on the Grants, by burning their houses, driving them off the land. These were cruel things to do, for many of the Yorkers were honest people who had been deceived by the big Yorker speculators into paying for their farms, even though the ownership of the land was in doubt. But most to blame of all for this state of affairs was the King of England and his advisors, who were trying to rule a distant country they knew nothing about. This double sale of land was a good example of their ignorance.

Ethan Allen, together with several of his brothers and Thomas Chittenden bought forty-five thousand acres of land on the Grants along the banks of the Onion River, later called the Winooski. They advertised for genuine settlers, people who would clear land and make farms.

Meanwhile, they built small log forts in order to defend the place against Yorkers. While they were engaged in putting up the forts, one of the Green Mountain Boys came to Ethan with word that a Yorker surveyor was on the Grants, running his lines. This was the same Cockburn whom Allen had run off before. Ethan blew up.

46

"Blast his malicious soul!" he roared. "Does he want more of us?"

Calling Remember Baker, Seth Warner, and a few more Boys, the party struck north from Bennington. When they came to Otter Creek, a handsome stream that flows into Lake Champlain, they were astonished to find several Yorker families had built cabins and a gristmill there. It had all happened in a few weeks.

John Reid was leader of the Yorker group, and the land Reid was on had also been bought by several of Ethan's friends. Ethan decided to act swiftly. Swooping out of the timber, he and his men drove Reid and the other settlers off the land, then broke the big millstones into pieces and threw them into the creek. Ethan stopped barely long enough to tell Reid that if any of the Yorkers dared to return here, their cabins would be burned. "And you alive in your cabins!" the fierce leader of the Green Mountain Boys promised.

Without halt Ethan continued northward and in the town of Bolton he and his Boys at last found Surveyor Cockburn and his gang. Attacking them with fury, they broke all the surveying instruments, then promised further violence should they return to the Grants. This time Cockburn got enough. He never did return.

But another Yorker surveyor, Benjamin Stevens,

47

did come — a tough and hardy man who had said that no Green Mountain Boys would drive him off the Grants. With him were several woodsmen and a bodyguard of Indians. He really meant business.

So did the Boys. Stevens hardly had his work started when his camp was attacked by Baker, Ira Allen and three other men in woodsmen's clothes. No guns were used. Baker leaped at Stevens, a large man, and threw him to the ground. Ira and another Boy jumped Steven's chief helper, and the three rolled into the campfire, where the Yorker's hair caught fire and started to burn. In five minutes all the Yorker party were prisoners, and tied to trees.

Now Baker stirred up the campfire in front of them, and he and the others sat around it, eating the Yorker provisions and drinking their rum.

"I reckon we ought to roast these fellers over this fire," Baker remarked.

Ira Allen agreed it would be a good idea. "Roast 'em good," he said, "and maybe they'll stay home in York, where they belong."

"Have to build the fire bigger."

"Lots of dry wood around here."

Surveyor Stevens and his men, bound fast to beech trees, began to sweat. Could it be possible that these savage backwoodsmen would carry out the threat? Now Remember Baker got up and stood

48

49

in front of his captives. "I guess I'll turn you loose this time," he drawled. "But if any of you is ever caught east of the lake, I'll roast you to a turn, every last one of you."

So saying he untied the Yorkers, gave them a little food, but not their guns or surveying instruments, and bade them begone.

As soon as Stevens and party had returned to Albany with the story of their capture, New York raised the reward on Ethan Allen's head to one hundred pounds, or about five hundred dollars. More than one Yorker sheriff tried to win it. One time two Yorker deputies found Ethan in a tavern near Manchester on the Grants. They thought he did not suspect who they were.

"Let's get him drunk," whispered one to his

fellow. "Then we can put him into our sleigh and take him to Albany. It will be easy."

They invited Colonel Allen to drink with them. They drank so much that the two Yorkers soon found themselves wobbly. Ethan laughed loudly. "Why, you stupid Yorker spies," he roared, "I have a little game to show you." He stood up, still sober and strong as an ox. Then he grasped each by his neck, lifted them from the floor, held them at arm's length and knocked their heads together with the sound of knocking on wood.

"Go back to your foolish governor," he cried. "Go tell him that Ethan Allen tried to knock your brains out but found you didn't have any." Then he tossed the two dizzy deputies out the tavern door and into the snow.

51

But far more serious events than these were shaping. It was now the fateful year 1775. Everywhere in the American Colonies there was a rising feeling against England, the mother country which, so the colonists felt, was taxing them heavily but allowing them nothing to say about their own government. King George came to be a hated name.

In 1775 the only representative of King George on the New Hampshire Grants was the King's Court, held at Westminster. On March 14 this court was to be held. The times were very bad. Settlers owed money they could not pay. Fearing they would be evicted from their farms, about one hundred men and boys took possession of the King's courthouse in Westminster on the night before the court was to open.

Hearing of this, Sheriff Paterson, hired by the English Crown, raised a posse of twenty-five armed men and marched to the courthouse. He ordered the anti-court party to come out of the building. They refused. Sheriff Paterson stationed his men, then shouted, "I will give you just fifteen minutes to get out of there. I order you out in the King's name. If you do not come out, I'll blow a lane through you!"

Just then Judge Chandler came on the scene. He calmed both sides, telling the anti-court party

they might remain in the courthouse until morning, if they wished. He also told the sheriff and his men to go home.

Leaving a small guard in the building, the anticourters went away. And all might have gone well had it not been for the sheriff's deputies, who got to drinking too much rum in John Norton's tavern near the courthouse. Then, later, filled with grog, they set out to attack the courthouse, approaching with stealth.

It was night, but a bright moon shone down on the impending tragedy. A sentry in the courthouse door was alert. The moonlight tipped the bayonets and pikes of the deputies as they marched. The sentry's sharp eye caught the glint on the steel.

For a moment the sentry could not decide what

to do, then he quietly waked his sleeping comrades
within the building, and came forth to challenge
the approaching party. "Who goes there?" he called
out. No answer came, but the deputies advanced.
All was now ready.

The drunken sheriff at the head of his gang
staggered up the courthouse steps. "Halt!" ordered
the sentry, and pushed the sheriff back.

Again the official swaggered to the platform.
This time the sentry and his comrades set upon the
drunken man with their clubs. The sheriff fell
back. He was beside himself with rage. He called
to his men.

"Fire!" he cried. "Fire, you bullies, fire!"

The night flashed red, and the thunder of gunfire
broke the stillness of the little town.

56

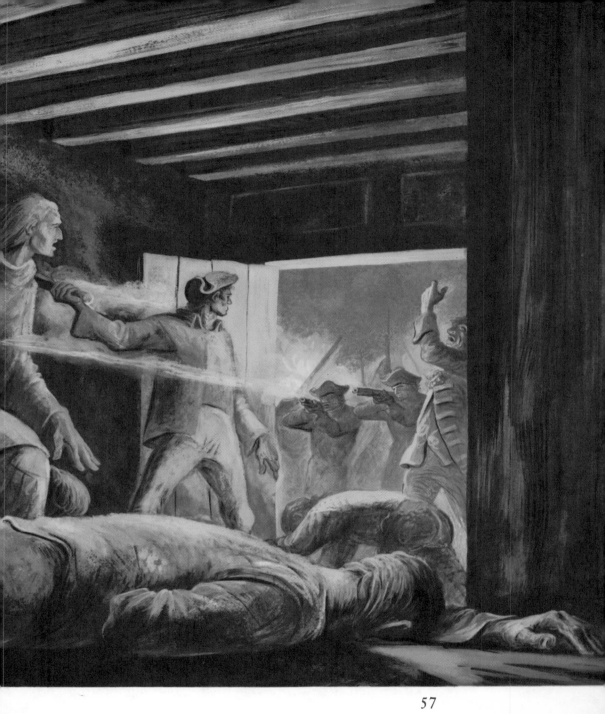

Inside the courthouse, William French, a young man of Brattleboro, went down with a ball through his head and four other wounds. Ten others of the anti-court party fell wounded. The courthouse floor ran red.

The Westminster Massacre was over.

News traveled fast and in all directions that night. Next day one hundred Green Mountain Boys, led by Lieutenant Robert Cochran, arrived in Westminster after an all-night's march. They patroled the village to keep order and also took part in the funeral of young French, who was buried with honors and declared to be a martyr in the war against New York and King George. In a little while, loving hands made a stone to mark his grave, and etched a few lines against the King of England:

58

Here William French his Body lies
For Murder his Blood for Vengeance cries
King Georg the Third his Tory crew
tha with a bawl his head Shot threw
For Liberty and his Country's Good
He lost his Life his Dearest blood.

The so-called Westminster Massacre proved to be the most important event that had happened on the Grants. It fired the people there with a great resolve to throw off New York's rule of their region. It also urged them on to join with the other colonies in their quarrel with England.

A little more than a month after the trouble at Westminster, word came to the Catamount Tavern in Bennington that the colonists of Massachusetts had taken up arms and fought two battles with the

King's soldiers at Lexington and Concord.

This was exciting news, and no one was more moved by it than Colonel Ethan Allen of the Green Mountain Boys. With members of his regiment, and other men of the Grants, he discussed what they might do to help the revolt of the American colonies.

One night in May, talk in the Catamount went on into the late hours, long after the rest of Bennington had gone to bed. And it was morning when the tallest man in the room stood up and pounded his fist on the table. "Boys," he said, "I think we should cross the lake and capture Fort Ti." Then he went to bed.

Colonel Allen referred to Fort Ticonderoga, one of the most famous military posts in America. It stood on a bold point overlooking Lake Champlain and was defended by British troops.

Next day after the night-long discussion in the Catamount, Ethan's brother, Heman, riding a tired horse, arrived at the tavern from Connecticut. "I've got important news for you," he told the tall colonel, and the two retired to a private room.

"Ethan, I've been sent to you by the Colonial authorities at Hartford. They want some help."

"We're ready. All we need to know is how to help."

"The men at Hartford wonder if you can raise enough Green Mountain Boys to take Fort Ti.

60

Can you possibly do it?"

"Take Ti? Why, that's what we were talking about all last night."

"You can do it, then?"

"It will take a few hours to get my men together, but I shall send messengers out at once."

"Do you know how many soldiers guard the fort?"

"No, I don't. But I can find out. I'll send a spy there."

"If you can take Ti, it will give great courage to all Americans."

"We are the lads to do it. Now let me get the word to the back country farms." With no fuss, Colonel Allen called half a dozen of his Boys in Bennington, told them to mount and ride. "Say that it is going to be the biggest wolf hunt of all,"

62

he said, briefly but forcefully.

Away went the messengers.

One of them went on foot because he had no good horse. He was Gershom Beach, a mighty man when it came to traveling swiftly through the woods. Beach ranged like a moose through seven towns, rousing the Boys on their farms, telling them that Ethan Allen was in need of help, and to hurry.

Back in Bennington, Colonel Allen, together with sixty-odd Green Mountain Boys and some fifty men who had just arrived from Connecticut, said good-bye to the Catamount and started north for Castleton, near Lake Champlain.

As they moved along the muddy trails, Ethan paused here and there to sound the call. His voice was like the deep boom of a war drum, savage and

vibrant, that echoed against barn and forest and pounded its way through the chinked logs of cabins, through cedar roofs, through the toughest homespun, right to a man's heart.

"We are going on a big wolf hunt!" cried Ethan Allen.

Colonel Allen knew these backwoodsmen and they knew him. His call was magic, and they rallied to it. At Arlington plows were left in their furrows, and men got into buckskin to take down their long guns and join the marching column.

It was the same at Manchester, at Dorset, at Pawlet, at Poultney. Grim-faced farm women, brown as squaws from the constant smoke in their cabins, hurriedly molded bullets at fireplaces. Boys and girls filled horns with powder. Children cried,

64

dogs barked, horses whinnied, and the mob of marching men grew steadily greater as it moved northward.

"A big wolf hunt!" shouted Ethan Allen again.

When they came to Castleton the army went
into camp, while Colonel Allen and the Connecticut
leaders thought over the best method of attacking
the fort across the lake. Ethan needed to know
first how many soldiers were in the big bastion.

"Noah Phelps!" Ethan called to one of the younger
Boys.

"Yes, Colonel?"

"Noah, can you get into Fort Ti — and out
again?"

"I think I can, sir."

"We must know how many troops are there."

"I understand, sir. Let me try."

"Away with you, then. And try to learn anything else about the fort that might be of value to
us."

"Yes, sir."

The young man turned and disappeared into the
woods toward the lake.

Boats must be had to transport the little army.
Colonel Allen sent out two parties to find such craft
as they could. They were back by nightfall with
a huge scow and two big rowboats. These would
have to do.

In the evening, too, back from Fort Ti came
young Phelps. He went to Colonel Allen.

"There are not more than fifty soldiers there,"
he reported.

"Fine!" said Ethan. "Fine! And what else did
you learn?"

"A part of the outer wall, sir, is beginning to fall
down."

"Which portion, Noah?"

Young Phelps took a stick and traced an outline

66

of the fort in the ground, while Ethan watched closely. "The wall is weak here," said Phelps. "And here, at the South Curtain, it has crumbled and fallen. It is quite a breach."

"Good work, my lad," Ethan complimented young Noah. "You have performed a brave act and the Green Mountain Boys are in your debt." This was high praise from Colonel Allen, and Noah Phelps was too happy to speak.

All was nearly ready for the voyage across the lake when a new soldier appeared on the scene. He said his name was Benedict Arnold and that he was a colonel sent by Massachusetts to command the expedition against Ticonderoga. He was dressed in a fine uniform. Epaulets sparkled from his

67

shoulders. A great plume waved from his cocked hat. He was proud in his manner. He seemed to take for granted that these rude backwoodsmen would be happy to accept him as their leader.

Colonel Arnold was mistaken. The Boys began to mutter, saying that Allen was their leader and they would serve under no other. One of the Boys shouted, "Let's hang him!"

Nor did Colonel Allen like the gaudy stranger.

"Sir," he said bluntly, "I am colonel of this crew and I propose to lead the expedition."

"But I, sir, am a military man. I have a commission."

"My commission was conferred on me by the Green Mountain Boys, which is authority enough in these parts."

They argued briefly, and Allen would not give in. He said that, as a matter of courtesy, he would permit Arnold to march with him at the head of the column, but he would not be in command.

The night was getting on. They must leave soon if they were to attack the fort just before daylight, which was Colonel Allen's plan. So eighty-three men got into the scow and boats, leaving Lieutenant Seth Warner in command of those who could not go in the first contingent.

Brisk winds from the north made a choppy sea. The night was fast turning into the gray of morning,

and the oarsmen put all their strength forward to
gain time on daylight. Colonel Allen warned everyone to be quiet, and the wallowing ships of war,
waves breaking over the bows, crossed the lake and
landed at Willow Point, just out of sight of the
fortress.

Ethan now formed his men into ranks, gave a low-
voiced command and his army of eighty-three,
equipped with almost every sort of weapon from
blunderbuss to squirrel gun — with a few armed only
with pikes and hunting knives — moved up the hill.
No lights could be seen. No sound came from the
fort that loomed up so tall and black and sinister in
the morning dusk.

Skirting the east wall, the column came to the
south wing, which Noah Phelps had noted was

70

partly in ruins. Without a word or a halt Colonel
Allen clambered over the broken wall, drawing his
long sword, and rushed head-on at a sentry, who
was dozing. That surprised soldier did what he
could. He leaped to his feet and aimed his musket.
"Halt!" he cried.

Colonel Allen came on fast. The sentry pulled
the trigger. There was a flash in the pan, but no
explosion.

The sentry turned and ran into the parade ground,
shouting warning. Colonel Allen was right on his
heels, and after Allen came his army.

In another moment the fort was a riot of noise
and movement. As the attackers swarmed into the
place, one brave but careless redcoat came out of
the guardroom to lunge at one of the invaders with
his bayonet. Without a word Colonel Allen fetched
the redcoat a terrific swipe with the flat of his sword,
felling him.

"Quarter! Quarter!" he begged.

"Get up!" roared Colonel Allen. "Get up and
take me to your commander!"

The fallen man got to his feet and led the way to
a short flight of stairs. "Up there, sir," he said.

With a leap like a catamount, Allen started up
the stairs.

"Come out of there, you British so-and-so's!" he
shouted like thunder.

71

As he spoke the door opened, revealing an officer. He was Lieutenant Jocelyn Feltham, second in command of the fort. He was a brave man, too, and he remained cool in the face of Allen, the gigantic figure with the big, threatening sword.

The stairs were swarming with Green Mountain Boys. Lieutenant Feltham, amazed and alarmed at this strange crew suddenly in his fort, looked Allen in the eye. "By what authority," he demanded to know, "have you entered His Majesty's fort?"

It was then that Ethan Allen delivered himself of one of the most famous lines in American history.

"In the name of the Great Jehovah and the Continental Congress!" he roared.

It was a resounding declaration, one no American ever will forget, and it must have astonished Lieutenant Feltham beyond words. When he could speak and move, he led the terrible Colonel Allen to the fort's commander, Captain Delaplace, who formally surrendered and ordered his men to parade without arms. Fort Ticonderoga had fallen to the Americans.

It was now broad daylight, and boats were bringing Allen's rearguard across the lake. Lieutenant Seth Warner and his men immediately made an attack on Crown Point, a much smaller British fort than Ticonderoga, and took it without a shot. Within

the space of a few hours, these backwoodsmen, the
Green Mountain Boys, had taken two British strong-
holds, together with prisoners and a large number
of cannon and whole boxes of flints, for use with
muskets.

Colonel Allen sent word by courier to Philadelphia
to notify the Continental Congress what he and his
brave men had done. He sent the British prisoners
under guard to Hartford, Connecticut. The news
of the bold exploit electrified the Americans everywhere, and gave them new and strong hearts for the
heavy fighting and the bitter years that lay ahead.

A little later, too, when the Americans under
General George Washington were besieging the
British in Boston, Colonel Henry Knox moved the
Fort Ti cannon overland to the American lines

75

around Boston. Here they were placed in position and their threat forced the huge redcoat army to leave the city and go to Canada. It was all a great victory for the colonists, and the groundwork for it had been laid by Colonel Allen and his Green Mountain Boys.

After such a remarkable victory as that at Ticonderoga, lesser men might have been inclined to sit back, to rest on their oars. But not Ethan Allen. He thought the Continental Congress was moving too slowly. He wanted more action. So he sat down and wrote a blood-tingling letter to them.

"I wish to God," he wrote, "America would at this critical juncture exert herself. She might rise on eagles' wings, and mount to glory, freedom and immortal honor, if she did now but know and exert her strength. Fame is now hovering over her head. I will lay my life on it, that with fifteen hundred men, and a proper artillery, I will take Montreal." Montreal was one of the biggest towns in Canada, strongly held by the British.

Congress took no action on Ethan's letter. But it did authorize enlistment of a regiment from the Grants in the Continental Army. To the surprise of almost everybody Seth Warner and not Ethan Allen was made colonel of the new regiment. It is probable that Ethan was not given command

76

because of his impatience with authority of any kind. He was a lone wolf, a man who worked best without orders from above.

Ethan may have felt hurt, but it did not dampen his patriotism. He worked hard to help Warner recruit the new regiment.

Now that he had no rank in any army, Ethan was on his own, the way he liked to be. Asking advice from nobody he set out for Quebec Province in Canada on as wild a mission as any man ever thought up. He would raise a few men himself, then attack and capture the important town of Montreal.

Dressed in buckskins, Ethan went down the Sorel River into enemy territory around Chambly. With him he had an interpreter, for these were mostly French-speaking people. Somehow he managed to gather a mob of some two hundred and fifty men, mostly farmers.

Meanwhile, Colonel Seth Warner and Major John Brown of the new Grants regiment were heading a scouting party in the vicinity. Ethan happened to meet them. They, too, were planning to attack Montreal.

"We can muster at least four hundred men," Major

Brown said. "And with your party, we should be able to take the city."

"I think we should attack from two different points," put in Colonel Warner.

"Before any attack, we must all get to the north side of the St. Lawrence river," Ethan pointed out.

"True," said Brown. "Let us cross the stream in the night, your men below the city, ours above. And both attack at sun-up."

"Aye," agreed Ethan with enthusiasm. "Take 'em by surprise from two directions. They'll think the whole American army is attacking."

The three men now set the date and the time, then parted. Ethan returned to his camp and called his men together, relating to them the plan. "Here's for Montreal," he cried, "or a turf jacket!"

Ethan Allen never was behind time in anything. Getting canoes, he moved his tiny army across the turbulent stream under cover of night. By morning he had landed one hundred and ten men on the Montreal side of the river.

Soon the sun started coming up, but no Major Brown and his army. Why they did not come has never been explained. But here was Ethan Allen and his mob, scarcely a real soldier among them. The sun mounted in the sky, while Ethan waited and fumed.

Now spies saw the strange crew by the river.

They hurried into the city to warn the British commander. Ten minutes later a regiment of five hundred well-armed soldiers came forth to meet the invaders.

After a hot, short battle, the British drove off or captured all the invading army, including Ethan Allen, who was taken under guard to the British commander. "Are you the Colonel Allen who captured Fort Ticonderoga?" demanded that red-coated person.

"I am that very man."

"Then, sir, you are the worst sort of rebel, a villain who deserves hanging."

"I did not come here to be abused, sir. I am an honorable prisoner of war."

"You are a scoundrel." The general shook his cane at Ethan, calling him vile names. Ethan stepped up close to the fuming officer and doubled up his great fist which he shook under the astonished Englishman's nose.

"By the gods of the hills, sir," he cried, his wild eyes flashing, "you will do well not to cane me, for I am not accustomed to it."

Brother officers calmed the general, and the hearing went on.

"I am not going to execute you — now," said the general. "I am going to send you to England, in chains, and there you will be properly hanged."

79

Ethan laughed in the officer's face, and was then led away. They loaded him with chains and put him into a black old hulk used as a prison ship.

Although the handcuffs put on Ethan were of the ordinary sort, the leg irons were huge. They weighed forty pounds and were attached to a bar of iron eight feet long. Ethan could lie down only on the flat of his back, a most uncomfortable position.

Sitting alone in the dark hold, in irons and chains, Ethan Allen thought and thought about the failure at Montreal. Why had not Major Brown's party arrived? He couldn't know, never did know.

The ship's doctor took particular delight in teasing the prisoner, telling him he was ripe for hanging. Once Ethan went into a fury at the doctor, and raising his handcuffs to his mouth, he set his strong teeth around the head of a large nail that was driven through the handcuff bar. He twisted it this way and that, in a frenzy, finally pulling out the spike with his teeth. Spitting out the nail, and throwing off the wrist shackles with a mighty heave, he stood erect in an effort to strike the doctor.

"You coward!" he roared, "if only I could lay hands on you!" But the leg irons held fast and the doctor escaped injury. The feat impressed Ethan's guards. "Zounds!" said one, "does this man eat iron?"

Elsewhere in the ship were thirty-four of Ethan's

men captured at Montreal.   For more than a month
the vessel wallowed across the Atlantic, finally land-
ing at Falmouth, England.   Here the prisoners were
taken off and paraded through town on the way
to their new prison, Pendennis Castle.   The event
was like a circus day.   Hundreds of English came
to see the first prisoners taken in the war with the
colonies.

The natives were astounded at the size and appear-
ance of Ethan Allen, the Yankee Colonel who had
captured their great fortress of Ticonderoga.   He
looked more like a gigantic savage than like a
military man.   He was still wearing a bright red
woolen stocking cap.   His hair, uncut for months,
tumbled down over his shoulders.   His jacket, of
fawnskin, was fringed at the bottom and along the

81

arms. He was a sensation in Falmouth.

Ethan was not brought to trial. Instead, after two weeks in the castle, he and several other prisoners were herded on board the frigate *Solebay*, part of a fleet that sailed first for Cork, Ireland.

At the Irish port, while Captain Symonds of the *Solebay* was absent on shore, a group of Irishmen came aboard to see the famous American prisoner.

"Are you, sir," asked the spokesman, "the gallant American colonel who captured the great Ticonderoga from the English?"

"I led my Green Mountain Boys to take that fort," admitted Ethan with pride.

"Then, sir," went on the Irishman, "it is my honor, on behalf of the people of Cork, to present you with these small tokens of our admiration."

He left an enormous package which Ethan found to contain a suit of clothes, tea, sugar, wine, a turkey, and two hats, one richly laced with gold. And just as the Irishmen were leaving, and when no guard was looking, one of the gentlemen of Cork slipped Ethan a fine dagger.

Little wonder the American was deeply touched by such hospitality. But when Captain Symonds returned to the ship, although he permitted Ethan to retain the clothing, he took away all the fine provisions. Ethan already had secreted the dagger.

Now, with several other ships, the *Solebay* set

out for America, carrying troops for Lord Cornwallis, the same commander who was later to surrender to General Washington at Yorktown.

When the fleet at last arrived at Cape Fear, on the North Carolina coast, Ethan and the other prisoners were removed, put aboard the *Mercury*, and taken to Halifax, Canada. Locked up in prison for a brief time, they were again put on a ship, this time a man-o'-war commanded by Captain Smith, who greeted Colonel Allen as an equal and had him eat at the captain's table. This unusual treatment of a prisoner warmed the old warhorse's heart. He soon had opportunity to repay Captain Smith.

Among the prisoners on board was a new man, one Captain Burk, who had been captured while commanding an American vessel. Burk seems to have been something of an adventurer. He had somehow learned of what was supposed to be a secret matter. One night Burk came to Ethan.

"Colonel Allen," said Burk almost in a whisper, "did you know that this ship is carrying thirty-five thousand pounds sterling?"

"I did not. What of it?"

"I have a plan. I can get certain members of the ship's crew to join with us. We will stage a mutiny, set free all the prisoners, take over the ship, kill the captain, and . . ."

"Hold, sir, hold," said Ethan, but Burk continued.

"Kill the captain, take over the ship and sail her into New York or Boston as a prize ship of war. It will free us and also make us wealthy."

"Captain Burk," said Ethan bluntly, "I will have no part in such a plan. I honor Captain Smith as a decent man."

"You won't join us?" Burk was scarcely able to believe his ears.

"Not only that, sir. Not only that, but I shall fight on Captain Smith's side, should you attempt such a plan."

The mutiny never came off, and thus did Ethan Allen, a bad enemy and a good friend, repay Captain Smith for his kindness.

Ethan Allen's last sea voyage came to an end at New York City late in October of 1776. That city was still in the hands of the British, and it wasn't long before a red-coated officer came to talk to Ethan privately in his cell.

"Colonel Allen, we English would be happy to offer you a commission in the King's Army."

Ethan said not a word. The officer continued.

"If you agree, you shall be freed at once. We will take you to England and there you shall be given a commission on the staff of General John Burgoyne, who is presently to sail for America with an enormous army."

84

"I am a Green Mountain Boy," replied Ethan, "and I should prefer to die a prisoner of you British than to serve you in any way."

"You are mad, sir, to talk like that."

"Mad, perhaps I am, but I am not a traitor."

The officer left in disgust.

For several long months Ethan remained in the New York prison. He was more restless than ever, for news came to him of how the Revolution was rolling along in fine style, while he was helpless and in prison. While he was confined, the battle of Bennington was fought on the Grants and many of his old Green Mountain Boys played heroic parts in driving the British back to Saratoga, where they were defeated in one of the great battles of the war.

Then, in May of 1778, Ethan was taken out of his cell and exchanged for a British colonel who had been captured by the Americans. Ethan was happy to be on what he called "Liberty Soil" once more. He was invited to visit General Washington, then in camp at Valley Forge, who found Colonel Allen to be a man "of great fortitude and firmness."

Stopping briefly in Philadelphia, Ethan wrote to Congress, saying that if the Americans had no need for officers, then he himself should be glad to enlist as a common soldier.

Riding next to Connecticut, Ethan discovered that

his brother Heman had died only the week before. Then he pressed on for Sunderland on the Grants, where Ethan's wife and family had been living. He found them well, if somewhat strange after his long absence, and they and the neighbors too were shocked to see little more than the shadow of the man who had taken Ticonderoga, if not Montreal. Those events were now three years in the past.

Since then, many things had happened. Ethan learned that the land where his home had stood was no longer the New Hampshire Grants but Vermont, not yet one of the United States, but a sort of independent republic, with no definite ties with anyone. Vermont's independence had been accomplished on June 4, 1777, while Ethan still lay in an English prison. The new name of Vermont had been proposed by the same Doctor Thomas Young who had loaned books to Ethan in his youth.

Congress had refused to recognize Vermont. New York, which had claimed Vermont, was now too busy with the big war to trouble with anything else. Ira Allen, Jonas Fay, and Thomas Chittenden had been running Vermont. They and others had drawn up a constitution which, among other things, prohibited slavery, the first of its kind in the United States; and Chittenden had been elected governor by an Assembly. Vermonters had done all this while helping to fight the Revolutionary War.

86

Now that he was home again, the Republic of Vermont made ready to welcome the hero of Fort Ticonderoga and leader of the Green Mountain Boys. The day was set and the place selected was naturally Bennington. Postboys were sent riding to carry the word to the most remote tavern and farm in the region, and into Connecticut, New Hampshire, and Massachusetts.

They came by the score, by the hundred; on foot, horseback, a few in wagons and chaises. You may be sure that all the old Green Mountain Boys came to honor their great leader.

88

On the first day of the celebration three salutes were fired from a cannon for Colonel Allen. And next day the piece was fired again.

"BOOM, BOOM, BOOM!" . . . fourteen times the gun roared and was echoed by the green hills — thirteen for the United States, one for Vermont.

A great deal of rum was drunk in the Catamount Tavern. A messenger to Colonel Allen came with a letter from General Washington, containing a colonel's commission in the United States Army; and with it back pay for all the time he had been in captivity.

It was doubtless the happiest day Colonel Allen had known since his Green Mountain Boys had taken Fort Ti.

Now that he was home again, Colonel Allen and his friends again turned to the problem of land ownership. They were determined that no Yorker could hold land there unless bought under a New Hampshire title.

The best way to do this, Colonel Allen believed, was to convince Congress that Vermont should be one of the United States. To this end Ethan now did a good deal of writing, arguing the subject in newspapers and pamphlets.

Governor Chittenden turned to Ethan to help in organizing a Vermont militia. The assembly voted

90

to draft men for it. A few towns, among them Putney, objected. Starting out with twenty men, Colonel Allen marched for Putney, and along the way sounded his battle cry. "Come on," he shouted at every farm. "Come, my boys, it's another wolf hunt."

The old magic was still in his cry, for along the line of march eighty more men joined the column, guns on their shoulders, to force Putney to do its share in the militia draft. Arrived in that village, Colonel Allen called the inhabitants together; and when they had assembled he gave them a terrible tongue-lashing, struck several with the flat of his sword, and arrested thirty-six on charges of defying the Republic of Vermont.

A little later, when the town of Guilford, filled with Yorkers, defied a Vermont sheriff sent to collect taxes, Colonel Allen again called his men together. Marching on Guilford in force, he arrested Timothy Phelps who claimed to hold a sheriff's commission from the *State of New York*.

Taken before Colonel Allen, who sat on a big black horse, Phelps began protesting immediately.

"I am the true sheriff here," he cried. "Vermont has no authority in this town. It is a New York town. And I tell ——"

Allen made no reply, but he acted. He quietly unsheathed his sword and when the pretended sheriff stopped for breath, Allen reached out and with one mighty swipe cut Phelps's hat neatly from his head.

"Take the foolish dolt away!" he roared, then galloped off to lecture the assembled townspeople, who were certain that the Devil himself had come to Guilford.

Sitting his big horse, Colonel Allen gave voice: "I, Ethan Allen, do declare that I will give no quarter to the man, woman, or child who shall oppose me. Do you hear?

"Further, unless the inhabitants of Guilford peacefully submit to the authority of Vermont, I swear I will lay it as desolate as Sodom and Gomorrah!"

It was a truly terrible threat, uttered by one whose very name was a terror to Yorkers. Ethan followed it by arresting twenty men whom he considered ringleaders and taking them to Westminster jail. Guilford gave Vermont no more trouble.

Meanwhile, Vermont was getting organized. Ira Allen, a man of many talents, devised a coat of arms for the state, used to this day. Plans were laid to set up a mint to make Vermont coins. Ethan was elected Brigadier-General of the Vermont Army. Provision was made for the governor's cabinet. Vermont even appointed an "ambassador" to treat with Great Britain and other foreign powers.

Ethan Allen's wife had died in 1783. A year or so later he married Frances Buchanan, a young

92

widow of Westminster. For a time they lived in Bennington, where printers were bringing out a book on philosophy Ethan had written.

Due to his long captivity, General Allen's health had begun to fail, and he no longer wanted to ride and raise riots. Now he planned his retirement. The war of the Revolution had just ended with the surrender of Cornwallis at Yorktown.

Brother Ira had been developing the Allen lands along the Onion River and was also founding the city of Burlington. Ethan had an interest in these lands, so, in 1787, he rode north and picked a site for his home on the pretty river. Ira lived near, operating a sawmill and a gristmill, and trading with Canada.

So Ethan built himself a house there and moved his family, which included three daughters by his first wife and two babies, Fanny and Hannibal, by his second. He also had two free Negroes as hired men. Here on the Onion, he said, he would live the rest of his life. It wasn't to be long.

The season of 1788 was a bad one in northern Vermont. All the settlers faced something not far from famine. The Allens managed to raise a little wheat and corn, but the hay crop had failed and they must have feed for their cattle. Knowing that hay had been good on South Hero Island, where Ebenezer Allen had a big farm, Ethan asked his cousin if he could spare a load. He could, and

93

gladly. Let Ethan come over for it.

Taking one of his Negro helpers, Ethan drove by ox team across the thick ice of Lake Champlain to the Island. It was the eleventh of February, and quite cold.

Ebenezer Allen was an old Green Mountain Boy who had been at Ethan's side at Fort Ticonderoga, and now he prepared for the coming of his famous relative. He invited all former Green Mountain Boys in the neighborhood to come and spend the evening at his place, with General Allen.

Milking was done early that night, and men on foot and in sleighs made their way to Ebenezer Allen's farmhouse. There was plenty to talk about, for old soldiers of all times and places are never without a topic for conversation.

Fort Ti had to be taken all over again. Yorkers had to be run off Vermont farms and so on. The hours passed swiftly. At about midnight General Allen felt he would like to lie down a while. To bed he went, but not for long. Before daylight he had roused the house, calling for his Negro man, his oxen, and his load of hay.

"But, Cousin Ethan," said Ebenezer, "there is no reason that you can't stay until daylight, and have breakfast before you go."

"Thanks, Cousin Eben, thanks," roared General Allen, "but we must be on the way. My cattle

are hungry. Good-bye.''

General Allen was hoisted up atop the load of hay. The Negro swished his goad-stick, and off they started.

At some point along the way, the Negro was frightened to see General Allen struggling violently. The devoted man was obliged to use force to hold him in the hay. General Allen was obviously very ill. The Negro hurried the oxen as much as possible, but by the time they arrived at the Allen home the general was unconscious.

Some twelve hours later, and without gaining consciousness for more than a few moments, Ethan Allen died. It was the cold twelfth of February, 1789.

There was a big funeral. All residents of the

95

neighborhood, and every old Green Mountain Boy in Vermont who got the news in time was present.

Muffled drums beat the way, and crossed swords were laid on the plain coffin of pine.

Old Governor Chittenden was there and marched every step of the way, acting as one of the pall-bearers. In fresh snow the column moved across the ice above the mill dam at Onion River falls. Every little way a halt was made and a small cannon fired.

On the brow of a hill overlooking the river the procession came to its last halt. The grave had been dug through ground frozen as hard as marble, in a small clearing in the forest.

The coffin was lowered into the ground, while three volleys of musketry were fired. Snow was falling while Major Goodrich spoke briefly, telling what General Allen had accomplished for his country and his state, and what he had suffered for them, too.

That was how they laid the old Green Mountain Boy away in the ground and snow came down that night so thick it covered the grave a foot deep.

Less than two years later, Vermont was admitted to the Union as the fourteenth state. Ethan Allen and his Green Mountain Boys had done their work well. The State of Vermont is their monument.

92
All   Holbrook, Stewart

           America's Ethan
           Allen

92
All

Holbrook, Stewart

AUTHOR

America's Ethan Allen

TITLE

DATE LOANED	BORROWER'S NAME	DATE RETURNED
2-13	Shane	24c